WORLD'S SCARIEST PLACES

EERIE RAILROADS

ALIX WOOD

Gareth Stevens
PUBLISHING

Please visit our website, **www.garethstevens.com**. For a free color catalog of all our high-quality books, call toll free 1-800-542-2595 or fax 1-877-542-2596.

Cataloging-in-Publication Data

Names: Wood, Alix.
Title: Eerie railroads / Alix Wood.
Description: New York : Gareth Stevens Publishing, 2020. | Series: World's scariest places | Includes glossary and index.
Identifiers: ISBN 9781538242537 (pbk.) | ISBN 9781538241998 (library bound) | ISBN 9781538242544 (6 pack)
Subjects: LCSH: Haunted places--Juvenile literature. | Ghosts--Juvenile literature. | Railroad stations--Miscellanea--Juvenile literature. | Railroad terminals--Miscellanea--Juvenile literature.
Classification: LCC BF1461.W64 2020 | DDC 133.1'22--dc23

First Edition

Published in 2020 by
Gareth Stevens Publishing
111 East 14th Street, Suite 349
New York, NY 10003

Produced for Gareth Stevens by Alix Wood Books
Designed by Alix Wood
Editor: Eloise Macgregor

Photo credits:
Cover, 1 background, 4 , 7, 8 top, 13, 17 top, 19 bottom, 21 top, 23 top, 26, 29 bottom © Adobe Stock Images; 1 porter © John Wen; 5 left © Imperial War Museum; 5 right © William Murphy; 6 inset © City of Vancouver Archives; 10 © William Archer Price; 11 top © Cemeteries.org.nz; 12 © Chloe93; 14, 15 © Roger Marks; 17 bottom © Ellgaard Holger; 18 © Zhen Kang; 20 top © Alexander Gardner; 22 © Abesty; 24 © Danielle Lupin; 25 © Mark Gonzalez; 27 © Baycrest/Wikipedia; 28 © Jonathan Warren; 29 © Wholtone; all other images are in the public domain

Printed in the United States of America

CPSIA compliance information: Batch #CS19GS. For further information contact Gareth Stevens, New York, New York at 1-800-542-2595.

Contents

Ghost trains and long-dead passengers can all be found haunting the world's railroad tracks. Why would ghosts haunt a railroad? Sometimes, constructing a station may have disturbed an old burial place. Perhaps ghosts were the victims of horrible rail accidents. There are even some creepy railroads that were specially built to transport the dead!

At night, on a long-abandoned rail line in Saskatchewan, Canada, a strange light is often seen. The light changes color and brightness as it travels along the path of the old track near the village of St. Louis. Some think it's the headlight of a ghost train. Others think the light is the lantern of a ghostly **decapitated** rail worker searching for his lost head!

Soldiers often traveled to war by rail. Connolly Station in Dublin, Ireland, was bombed during World War II. Since then, it is said to be haunted by ghostly soldiers. Once, a security guard monitoring platform 5's cameras saw two men in uniform appear on the screen. When he went to investigate the unused platform, the figures had vanished.

Empty station platforms can feel creepy. A lonely railroad platform at night can certainly send shivers down your spine!

Waterfront Station, Canada

This grand old station in Vancouver, Canada, was built in 1915. The station originally had hotel rooms, restaurants, and even a dance hall! Nowadays, most of the space is used as offices or for storage. Even so, night staff working in the station offices still bump into some of the ghostly old passengers there.

WATERFRONT STATION IN 1923

A guard saw a woman in 1920s clothes dancing to music in a station corridor one night. As he approached, the music stopped and the woman suddenly disappeared.

A security guard on patrol one night entered a room used to store desks. As he turned around to walk back out of the room, several of the old desks had silently moved to block the doorway! He had to quickly climb over the desks to escape.

When a night security guard shone his flashlight into an empty room at the station, he suddenly saw the glowing white face of an old woman. She reached out her arm toward him, with a look of sadness on her face. The terrified guard ran!

London Necropolis Railway, England

1850s, London, England. The capital's graveyards were full to bursting, and a recent cholera **epidemic** had left over 14,500 dead. A new railway line opened with a special, gruesome task. It was to carry corpses and mourners out of London to a new cemetery.

In **Victorian** England, some wealthy people did not like the idea of sharing a train with poor people! The railway managers had to keep different classes of the living and the dead separate, on and off the train!

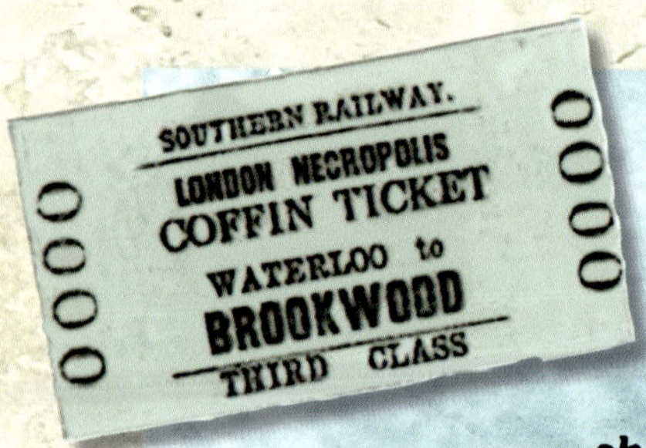

A first-class coffin ticket allowed a choice of plot and headstone. A second-class ticket got a limited choice of plot. A bit more money got a grave marker, but the plot could be reused! A third-class ticket had no choice of plot, and no marker. Any burial usually included two free return tickets for mourners, too.

This grand station entrance was where first- and second-class coffins were brought. Their families had private waiting rooms, and could watch the coffin being loaded on the train. Third-class families had to share a waiting room and could not see their coffin being loaded.

There were two stations at the cemetery. One was for Church of England burials, and the other station was for everyone else.

The Necropolis Railway must be the most ghostly train of all, as it carried so many dead bodies to their graves!

Otira Tunnel, New Zealand

Building a railway line can be dangerous and difficult. In New Zealand's Southern Alps, huge mountains blocked the railway engineer's path. A vast tunnel had to be built to link Otira with Arthur's Pass. The Otira tunnel is 5.3 miles (8.5 km) long. A dark tunnel can be scary enough, but it is even more scary if the tunnel is haunted!

The tunnel was started in 1908. The work was dangerous. Holes were drilled into the rock, and then filled with explosives. Each explosion inched the tunnel deeper into the mountain.

THE OTIRA TUNNEL ENTRANCE DURING CONSTRUCTION

A ghost has been seen walking beside the tracks. People believe the ghost may be a worker killed during the tunnel's construction. He is seen traveling east toward the port, carrying his belongings on his back. Perhaps he is trying to catch a ship home.

THE EASTERN TUNNEL ENTRANCE

This gravestone in a cemetery in Dunedin **commemorates** an English engineer who died after his arm got caught in machinery while building the tunnel. Could he be the ghost that haunts the railway line?

Union Station, Arizona

Once a busy railroad station, Union Station in Phoenix, Arizona, closed in 1995. It is now an office building. One passenger seems reluctant to leave, however. People working in the building have had some spooky encounters with a ghost they named "Fred."

Fred is believed to mainly haunt the attic. Workers sometimes feel a tap on their shoulder. When they turn around, no one is there! A shadowy figure also appears at the far end of the attic and then runs away. Some workers now refuse to enter the spooky attic at all!

The heavy side gate at the old station sometimes opens and closes repeatedly, all by itself!

In 1931, Union Station played a part in a gruesome double murder. Winnie Ruth Judd argued one night with two female friends and shot them both. She put their bodies in two large steamer trunks and headed to Union Station. She checked herself and her **grisly** luggage onto a train to Los Angeles!

Once in L.A., a porter noticed blood seeping out of the trunks. Judd was arrested and charged with murder. Her gruesome baggage was then shipped back to Union Station! Could the Union Station ghost have been one of the bodies in the trunks?

The ghost at Union Station appears as a shadowy, cold presence. It was given the name Fred because no one is sure if it is male or female, so Fred could be Frederica!

Leamington Spa Station, England

Not all railroad ghosts are scary. The railway station at Leamington Spa, England, has friendly ghosts. How do we know they're friendly? The station had so many reports of ghost sightings that the local railroad company hired a special **Supernatural Liaison** Officer! Nick Rees patrols the station and keeps contact with the station's ghosts. He believes his ghosts are friendly, and that they respect him.

Both passengers and station staff have experienced spooky events at the station. Ghosts have been seen waiting on the platforms. Footsteps can sometimes be heard along the empty station walkways, too!

On platform 3, there is a blocked stairway leading to an unused basement. This area is one of the most haunted areas of the station.

A SPOOKY PLATFORM AT LEAMINGTON SPA

The upstairs offices of the old station building are haunted, too. Staff working there experience doors slamming and their electrical equipment flickering on and off. Drawers open by themselves, paper is thrown around, and the staff sometimes hears creepy footsteps! You wouldn't want to work late at Leamington Spa!

Stockholm Metro, Sweden

Plenty of railroads have stories of ghost trains, but in Stockholm, Sweden, their ghost train is real! In 1965, Stockholm Metro bought eight unpainted wagons. People were used to the city's green trains. A strange, silver train pulling into an underground station late at night spooked passengers. The train became known as "Silverpilen" (the Silver Arrow).

Doors slid open on the outside of the train, and inside there were no advertisements or decorations. Often, the carriages were scratched, where graffiti had been removed. All this, and the unpredictable timetable of the carriages, made people wary of Silverpilen.

Stories began to spread about the silver train. People said if you boarded Silverpilen you could never get off it again. Some believed the train was only seen after midnight and was full of zombies! Many people were so afraid they wouldn't get on the silver carriages if they pulled in to the station.

Stockholm has a ghost station, too. The unfinished Kymlinge Metro station started to become linked with stories about Silverpilen. People believed the dead got on and off the train there!

Bishan MRT Station, Singapore

When you imagine a haunted railroad station, you probably picture an old, crumbling, spooky building with hundreds of years of history. So why is this modern metro station in Singapore so haunted? Perhaps because it was built on the site of an old Chinese cemetery.

Peck San Theng cemetery had more than 100,000 graves. When Bishan Metro Station was built on the site, the bodies were dug up and cremated. Could disturbing their resting place have caused angry spirits?

Several headless figures have been seen at the station. The ghost of a girl reportedly once boarded a train at Bishan Station. A terrified passenger then saw her remove her head and put it on the seat next to her! Headless passengers have also been seen walking the platforms and up the train aisles.

Construction workers building the station were spooked one night when a ghostly funeral procession headed along the tracks! Passengers also sometimes hear the sound of footsteps on top of the trains!

Railroad Track, Albany, New York

Assassinated President Abraham Lincoln's funeral train traveled from Washington, D.C., to Springfield, Illinois, in the spring of 1865. The phantom train is said to still travel the same route, at the same time, every year! It is often seen at midnight on April 27, on the railroad at Albany, New York. The air becomes cold, and clocks and watches are said to stop working. The train moves noiselessly, its black funeral drapes flapping silently at the sides of the ghostly carriages.

Lincoln's funeral train pulled nine carriages, draped in black. A photograph of Lincoln was attached to the front of the steam engine.

The ghost train is seen all along the 1,654-mile (2,661 km) journey. The track has been taken up on a section of line in New York State, but the ghost train has still been seen following the old route!

The funeral train did not just carry the body of the President. In 1862, Lincoln's 11-year-old son, Willie, died from **typhoid** fever. His body was removed from its grave in Georgetown and placed in a coffin on the train, so that he could be buried in Springfield with his father.

WILLIE LINCOLN

Macquarie Fields Station, Australia

This ordinary station on the outskirts of Sydney is a peaceful, happy place in the daytime. At night, the track is haunted by a terrifying ghost.

The ghost of a woman in a blood-stained white dress haunts the station. She sits or walks along the tracks, crying. The sound of sobbing or screaming can often be heard after the last train has left the station. Her ghost has also been seen wandering the platforms, staring into people's eyes!

The young girl that haunts Macquarie Fields is usually seen wearing an old-fashioned dancing dress.

AN AUSTRALIAN STEAM TRAIN

In 1906, a 43-year-old woman was run over by a steam train near Macquarie Fields station. Emily Georgeson had been unwell and was **depressed**. To cheer her up, a nurse took her to visit friends in nearby Glenfield. At the station, as the nurse was looking for their tickets, Emily quickly jumped on a train leaving for Macquarie Fields. Once there, she waited in a shed for a train, and then sadly threw herself in front of it. Could she be haunting the station?

Panteónes Metro Station, Mexico

Metro trains mostly travel in tunnels underground. There can be something a little scary about traveling in a dark tunnel. This spooky metro station on the outskirts of Mexico City is believed to be haunted, too.

You aren't the only person under the ground when you travel from this metro station! "Panteónes" means "graveyards" in Spanish. The metro station was built right next to two very large, old cemeteries.

THE ENTRANCE TO PANTEÓNES WITH THE CEMETERY IN THE BACKGROUND

Ghostly shapes have been seen in dark corners of the underground station. Could some of the cemetery residents be haunting the platforms?

There have been several mysterious happenings at Panteónes. People working at the station have heard footsteps seeming to come out of the walls.

The tunnel between Panteónes and the next station, Tacuba, is particularly haunted. Engineers working at night have heard loud screams and knocking sounds. Strange lumps also appear along the tunnel walls, which disappear as the workers get closer.

Caobao Road Subway Station, China

This Shanghai subway station is called the "Ghost Station" by locals because of its haunted **reputation**. Trains frequently stop working as they approach the platforms. When the engineers tow the broken train away from the station, it will suddenly work fine again. If a train manages not to break down, sometimes its doors will refuse to open instead.

Station cleaning staff have heard loud woman's laughter out of the darkness after the station is closed for the night. When they search the building, no one is there.

A young ghostly girl wearing a red dress has been seen sitting on one particular bench at the station. Her ghost appeared shortly after a young woman had been killed by a train there. Perhaps it is her ghost that the cleaners hear laughing late at night?

A man waiting on the platform at Caobao Road Station fell underneath an oncoming train to his death. This event is scary enough, but witnesses who saw it happen also said the man was either pushed or dragged by a strange, **inhuman** figure!

After mysterious deaths at the station, a glass shield with sliding doors now protects passengers from accidentally falling onto the tracks.

THE NEW SHIELDS AT CAOBAO ROAD

Cincinnati Subway Tunnels, Ohio

Under the streets of downtown Cincinnati there's a spooky abandoned subway system! The tunnels and station platforms were built but never used. Started in 1920, the project ran out of money and was abandoned in 1925 after only 2 miles (3.2 km) of underground tunnels had been built.

AN ABANDONED CINCINNATI SUBWAY STATION

People believe the tunnels may be haunted by the ghosts of workers who died while building the subway. Unexplained voices and footsteps have been heard down there.

A SEALED SUBWAY ENTRANCE

People have tried to think of uses for the abandoned tunnels. In the 1960s, Liberty Street station was converted into a nuclear bomb shelter, but was never used. The city used the tunnels to run a water main, and fiber optic cables. The ready-made tunnel was cheaper than digging a whole new trench, but the pipes and cables now get in the way of any future projects!

Some believe the real reason the tunnels were abandoned was because something **paranormal** lives down there! Some think a creature in the dark tunnels frightens away anyone who goes down there.

Glossary

assassinated when an important person is murdered by a surprise or secret attack

commemorates marks by a ceremony or a plaque

decapitated to have had the head cut off

depressed to be sad and low in spirits

epidemic a sudden, rapidly spreading outbreak

graffiti usually unlawful writing or drawing on a public surface

grisly gruesome

inhuman unlike what is typically human

liaison a person who sets up communication

paranormal events or phenomena that are beyond the scope of normal scientific understanding

reputation overall quality or character as seen or judged by people in general

supernatural relating to existence beyond the observable universe

typhoid a disease characterized especially by fever, diarrhea, weakness, headache, and an inflamed intestine

Victorian typical of the reign of Queen Victoria of England

Further Reading

Crosson Gilpin, Caroline. *National Geographic Readers: Abraham Lincoln (Readers Bios)*. Des Moines, IA: National Geographic Children's Books, 2014.

Williams, Dinah. *Creepy Stations (Scary Places)*. New York, NY: Bearport Publishing, 2013.

Website

Ducksters biography of Abraham Lincoln
http://www.ducksters.com/biography/uspresidents/abrahamlincoln.php

Publisher's note to educators and parents:
Our editors have carefully reviewed these websites to ensure that they are suitable for students. Many websites change frequently, however, and we cannot guarantee that a site's future contents will continue to meet our high standards of quality and educational value. Be advised that students should be closely supervised whenever they access the Internet.

Index

Don't be scared! Most people don't believe ghosts are real at all. No one has ever scientifically proven they exist. But it can be fun to get yourself a little spooked!